MUSCLE CARS
Thunder and Greased Lightning

Michael Benson

SMITHMARK

This edition published in 1996 by
SMITHMARK Publishers, a division of U.S. Media Holdings, Inc.,
16 East 32nd Street, New York, NY 10016.

SMITHMARK books are available for bulk purchase for sales promotion and premium use.
For details write or call the manager of special sales,
SMITHMARK Publishers, 16 East 32nd Street, New York, NY 10016; (212) 532-6600.

This book was designed and produced by
Todtri Productions Limited
P.O. Box 572, New York, NY 10116-0572
FAX: (212) 279-1241

Printed and bound in Singapore

ISBN 0-7651-9628-X

Author: Michael Benson

Publisher: Robert M. Tod
Editorial Director: Elizabeth Loonan
Book Designer: Mark Weinberg
Production Coordinator: Heather Weigel
Senior Editor: Edward Douglas
Project Editor: Cynthia Sternau
Assistant Editor: Linda Greer
Picture Researcher: Laura Wyss
Typesetting: Command-O, NYC

Photo Credits

Ron Kimball Studios
7 (top), 8-9, 14, 15, 17, 18 (top), 19 (bottom), 24-25, 26, 27, 28 (top & bottom), 29, 31, 33 (bottom), 34, 35, 36, 37, 40-41, 42 (top & bottom), 46, 47, 48, 49 (top & bottom), 50, 54, 58, 62, 69 (center), 70 (bottom), 71 (top & bottom), 74, 75 (top), 77 (top)

Cindy Lewis Photography
4-5, 6, 10, 12 (top & bottom), 13, 16, 30, 32, 33 (top), 38, 39, 43, 45, 56-57, 60, 61, 67, 68 (top & bottom), 69 (top), 70 (top), 73

Nicky Wright
7 (bottom), 18 (bottom), 19 (top), 20 (top & bottom), 21, 22 (top & bottom), 23, 44 (top & bottom), 51, 52, 53 (top & bottom), 59 (top & bottom), 63, 64, 65 (left & right), 69 (bottom), 72, 75 (bottom), 76, 77 (bottom), 78, 79

CONTENTS

INTRODUCTION

Once upon a time, a car was expected to be more than a mode of transportation—it was an extension of the driver's persona, a projection of the inner psyche, a style statement, a declaration of strength.

During the 1960s—and a little bit of the '70s—the automobile manufacturers of Detroit took advantage of America's lust for speed and style. They made cars that were designed not just to get their passengers from one place to another. They were designed to get them there *fast* and to *look good doing it*! In those great days of American high performance, a new car owner could conceivably drive his car out of the showroom and directly onto the racetrack. (Most, however, preferred to tinker with their cars a bit before they raced them.)

Back to the South Road Strip

In my neck of the woods, south of Rochester, New York, getting a new car during the muscle car era meant two things: Cruising it through town until everyone had seen it at least five times, and taking it out to the South Road strip to "see what it's got." So let's go back to the days when our hair was thicker and the night was longer; that blissful time, before the "energy crisis," when cars had some serious get-up-and-go, and when gas was plentiful and cheap—who cared if the cruising machine was thirsty?

Back in those days, street racing was a national sport rife with glory. But this lust for speed meant sad times too, as every town had its equivalent of "Dead Man's Curve."

Those who survived look at the power potential of today's measly domestic cars as pathetic, something "merely practical." Compared to the muscle cars, the cars coming out of Detroit today look like toys. Muscle cars aren't toys. Some men *still* think of them as women. They make them roar like thunder and drive them faster than greased lightning.

Muscle Cars: Thunder and Greased Lightning is a tribute to those cars, a nostalgic look at the days when patches of rubber were burned onto pavement under every stoplight in the country.

This book will examine the history of muscle cars and take a detailed look at a few of the best gas guzzlers in automotive history. Plus, readers will meet modern-day mechanics who have restored aging muscle cars to their original beauty and power.

Enjoy!

The 1962 Impala Convertible featured the same "409" engine that the Beach Boys sang about, and that year it was new and improved, with a single carburetor and 380 horses.

The 1968 Oldsmobile convertible offered sleek lines, and looked best with the fire-engine-red paint job.

The 1970 Buick GS Stage 1 had the look of a muscle car, but many thought that, considering the car's weight, the 350-cubic-inch engine lacked the desired power.

FOLLOWING PAGE: Twenty thousand 1963 Corvette Sting Rays were sold in 1963. The cost at the time was about $4,300. This car's slick fastback was controversial because it had a split window in the rear. Though it looked great, the divider bar sometimes caused the driver to have dangerous blind spots.

The 1968 1/2 Mustang Cobra Jet introduced to the line of pony cars the 427-cubic-inch engine worth a sizzling 335 horses.

The 1957 Chrysler 300C convertible came with a Hemi engine—that's short for hemispherical cylinder head. The engine increased power by increasing volumetric and thermal efficiency.

CHAPTER ONE

THE 1960s

The muscle car became an inevitability in 1951 when Chrysler introduced the 331-cubic-inch Hemi (hemispherical cylinder head) engine. With a little garage work, the powerplant could produce 350 horsepower. A drag-strip mechanic could modify that up to an astounding 1,000 horsepower.

Under the hood of Chrysler 300s, the Hemi engine gathered checkered flags on the stock-car circuit of the mid-'50s like it was gathering bugs on the windshield.

When Chrysler put the Hemi into a hot-looking convertible called the Chrysler 300, modern mythology was written. The 1955 Chrysler 300 tore up every big stock-car track in the country. Without the Hemi and the Chrysler 300, the muscle car craze of the 1960s and early 1970s would have been very different.

The Ford Shelby Cobra

Beginning in 1962, car designer Carroll Shelby set out to make a street car that looked and ran like a European race car. The result was the Ford Shelby Cobra. The Cobra had a monstrous engine; with a car of this weight, the effect is very much like attaching the driver to a rocket.

The 1966 Ford Shelby Cobra was the fastest American-made street car of all time: With a 427-cubic-inch engine producing 425 horsepower, it ran a quarter mile in a little more than 12 seconds—a speed of 118 miles per hour. No American factory car has ever been faster.

The 1965 version was the first to offer the 427 engine, but its body design at that time was too small for the huge engine to fit. A new body had to be built to accommodate the mega-powerplant, so the 1965 Cobras with the 427 were 5 inches longer than Cobras with smaller engines in them. The extra 5 inches sure didn't slow this car down. Although not quite as fast as the next year's model, the '65 is said to have gone from a full stop to 100 miles per hour, then back to a full stop again in 13 seconds.

The line was discontinued in 1967. Today, these cars are so rare and so highly cherished by enthusiasts that a seller could name his price. Muscle car purists, however, don't go for cars this light. Power is the key, and power is based on more than speed—it's also based on momentum!

The Shelby Cobra's 427-cubic-inch engine, in all of its glory!

Even the front dash of the 1965 Shelby Cobra 427 SC looked fast!

The 1965 Shelby Cobra was the first to offer the 427 engine, but its body design at that time was too small for the huge engine to fit. A new body had to be built to accommodate the mega-powerplant so that 1965 Cobras with the 427, like this one, were 5 inches longer than Cobras with smaller engines.

Muscle Truck?

What was the most outrageous muscle car ever? How about a muscle car that was part pickup truck? The 1959 El Camino from Chevrolet was the most intense blend of pickup utility, passenger car design, and muscle ever seen.

Chevy introduced the El Camino in 1959 and 1960, with a futuristic design based on the Bel Air. It had thin roof pillars, thin air scoops at the front of the hood, and big fins at the rear. The El Camino had the room to carry a lot of stuff, but it didn't have the strength to haul it. The maximum load was only 1,200 pounds, and even that weight was haulable only if you bought several options, such as the oversized tires and the heavy-duty rear springs.

The original El Camino came in two models. One came with a six-cylinder, 235-cubic-inch engine generating 135 horsepower, and the other had a V-8 power-plant available in either 290-horsepower or 335-horsepower versions.

The initial attempt at the El Camino was not popular, and it was discontinued after 2 years. But it came back in 1964, this time with more muscle under the hood—a lot more muscle.

This time around, the El Camino was based on the Chevelle station wagon rather than the Bel Air, and the marketing department advertised the new version as a personal truck, emphasizing how much fun it was rather than how functional it could be. The original El Camino had had a drab interior designed for work. The new version had the color and trim suitable for driver and passenger enjoyment.

By 1965, the El Camino could be purchased with Chevrolet's hottest engine under the hood: the Corvette engine—a fuel-injected V-8 capable of 360 horsepower. That's muscle!

In 1966, Chevrolet introduced an option that put even more power under the hood. Four years later, the El Camino featured a new 400-cubic-inch engine rated at 330 horsepower. Optional were two new versions of the 454-cubic-inch monster, potentially worth 450 horsepower.

Like other muscle cars, the El Camino's power numbers shrank when the price of gas rose in the early 1970s. And with the shrinking of the line's power came a shrinking of its popularity.

Ford introduced its bold new Ranchero pickup in 1957, the first vehicle in twenty years to be a full-fledged hybrid of car and truck. The idea, which would be repeated by Chevrolet a few years later in the form of the El Camino, was to combine pickup utility with car style. By 1971, the Ranchero still wasn't a car and it wasn't a truck, but it had muscle galore in the form of the big Ford Cobra Jet 428 engine.

The 1967 model was the last of the line for the Shelby Cobra. This is the 427, but sales during that final year showed that the 428 was the more popular version.

The American GTO

The original American GTO, the Pontiac Tempest GTO, was introduced in 1964. Available as an option was a 389-cubic-inch engine with special HO heads, a high-lift cam, and high-performance valve springs.

Those who drove the four-barrel version of the 1965 Pontiac GTO got a whopping 335 horsepower, while those who invested in the "Tri-Power" option could boost that to 360. The "Tri-Power" option had three Rochester two-barrel carburetors in a row. For street driving, only the center carb functioned; put the pedal to the metal and the outer two kicked in, readying the driver for the strip. Also making its factory debut in this car was the Hurst shifter, which came as an option.

The 1968 Pontiac GTO was the winner of *Motor Trend* magazine's "Car of the Year" award—and for good reason. The body was all new from the '67 version, sleeker with horizontal headlights, an Enduro bumper, and functional hood scoops. The optional 400-cubic-inch "Ram Air" engine was rated at 360 horses. It was updated mid-season and renamed "Ram Air II."

This car is considered the first full-sized muscle car. The name caused controversy at first, though. The GTO designation was borrowed from Ferrari; it originally stood for *Gran Turismo Omologato* (Great Tour Ratifier). This bothered sports car purists. The furor only died down after *Car and Driver* magazine proclaimed that this GTO—with its ability to go from a full stop to 100 miles per hour in a little under 12 seconds—was every bit as hot as its Italian counterpart.

The 1964 Pontiac GTO sold 32,000 units, a record among Pontiac's first-year models.

Anyone who drove the four-barrel version of the 1965 Pontiac GTO convertible got a whopping 335 horsepower. Those who invested in the "Tri-Power" option could boost that to 360.

A classic "Goat," the 1968 GTO ragtop was the first American machine to feature the Hurst-shifter as a factory-fitted option.

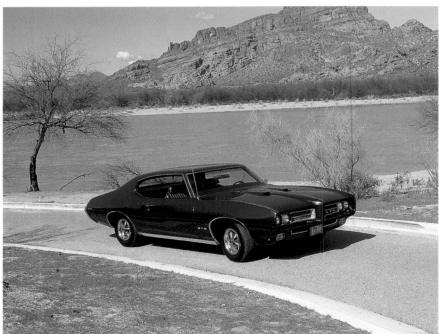

The 1969 Pontiac GTO sold 72,287 units. This number was not as large as the year before, but almost twice as large as the year after.

The sleek black interior of the 1969 Pontiac GTO, the year that the "Goat" peaked in popularity.

The 1964 Pontiac GTO is consider by many to be the first full-sized muscle car. It was actually the old Pontiac Tempest with a 389-cubic-inch V-8 engine under the hood. The GTO was the concept of advertising man Jim Wangers and John Z. DeLorean.

The 1968 Plymouth Road Runner had a simple bench seat and an austere vinyl interior. No luxuries. Just power. And the horn went, "Beep beep!"

Standard for the 1968 Plymouth Road Runner was a 383-cubic-inch engine souped up to rate 335 horsepower. There was a 426-cubic-inch Hemi engine option (425 horsepower) that came with necessitated structural reinforcements—an upgrade of the suspension and drivetrain.

The 1968 Plymouth Road Runner

"Beep-beep." That's the way the Road Runner's horn sounded. It was a car for young people—with an advertising campaign aimed directly at the youth market.

That's because the Road Runner was affordable for young people. Other cars with enough muscle to appeal to youth were being built with so many luxuries that they had out-priced a large segment of their market. The Road Runner had a simple bench seat and an austere vinyl interior. There were no luxuries, just power.

The ad campaign even bragged about the Road Runner's lack of frills: "The entire structure is of unitized construction, and marked by an absence of exterior frills and ornamentation. Even the rear windows are simple swing-out units that offer additional savings in weight over roll-up types."

Standard for the Road Runner was a 383-cubic-inch engine, which could be souped up to rate 335 horsepower. There was a 426-cubic-inch Hemi engine option (425 horsepower) that necessitated structural reinforcements—an upgrade of the suspension and drivetrain. This was the model that always outran that pesky coyote.

The Road Runner was a seriously feared automobile. Because it lacked luxuries, it was extremely light, and its power-to-weight ratio was very high. It had a wheelbase that was 116 inches long, and an overall length of 202.7 inches. The overall width was 76.4 inches; it stood 52.5 inches high and weighed 3,405 pounds.

All of this was at an affordable price which spelled popularity for the new model—44,598 Road Runners were sold in 1968; of those, 1,011 were Hemi-equipped.

The 1968 American Motors Company AMX

Craig Breedlove was a famous speed racer during the 1960s. For many years, Breedlove held the land-speed record driving a rocket car known as the "Spirit of America." He was the first man to travel 600 miles per hour without going airborne. In 1968, he chose the AMC AMX (the initials stood for American Motors Experimental)—which he, of course, had modified—and drove it to 106 speed records at the Goodyear test facility.

For regular folks, the most power available in the AMX came with the "Go" package, which offered a 390-cubic-inch engine. The power options for the 1968 AMX included the big 390-cubic-inch V-8, which produced 315 horsepower. The 390 was top-of-the-line for the AMX through 1970.

Craig Breedlove set 106 speed records in the American Motors AMX. For regular folks, the most power available in the 1970 AMX came with the "Go" package, which offered a 390-cubic-inch engine.

A front-right view of the fast-moving 1969 Dodge Daytona Charger.

The 1969 Dodge Daytona Charger was the car that broke the 200-mile-per-hour at the Talladega Superspeedway in Talladega, Alabama—with the legendary Buddy Baker behind the wheel.

The powerplant of the 1969 Dodge Daytona Charger was a 440-cubic-inch Hemi.

Until the release of the 1968 AMX, American Motors had been losing money. They needed to improve their image with a fast car, and the AMX was it. The AMX was introduced to the public in February 1968 at the Daytona International Speedway. Two weeks later it caused a stir at the nation's largest auto show in Chicago.

The AMX was the first two-passenger, steel-bodied, production-type sports car to be seen since the 1957–58 Ford Thunderbird. A brother to the Javelin, the AMX was built with a 97-inch wheelbase version of the Javelin's frame. Only 6,725 AMX Series 30 cars were built; they were sold at an introductory price of $3,245.

The 1969 Dodge Daytona

You couldn't miss the Daytona. It was shaped like a rocket and had a huge wing on the back. The body was an aerodynamically enhanced version of the previous year's Dodge Charger, with a scientifically designed 19-inch nosepiece attached to the front. This was the car that broke the 200-mile-per-hour barrier at the Talladega Superspeedway in Talladega, Alabama—with the legendary Buddy Baker behind the wheel.

Both engine options featured Hemi engines, sized at 440 and 426 cubic inches. Dodge, it is apparent, never had any ambition to sell a lot of Daytonas to the public. It was designed to be a big-league stock car. The minimum production run to qualify a model for the NASCAR (National Association of Stock Car Auto Racing) circuit was 500; Dodge produced 503 Daytonas.

FOLLOWING PAGE: Dodge issued an update of their Dodge Daytona in 1969 called the 1969 1/2 Daytona "Wingthing." This version was twenty percent more aerodynamically clean than its predecessor.

*The Dodge Charger Daytona continued
to win big on the NASCAR circuit in 1970.*

The Chevrolet Chevelle

The 1964 Chevrolet Chevelle had a muscle look, but no giddyup under the hood. The following year, that all changed. The 1965 Chevelle lived off of a 396-cubic-inch powerplant that cranked out 375 horses—so much power that the frame needed to be strengthened and new stabilizer bars added to compensate for the extra torque.

The 1966 Chevelle SS (Super Sport) still had the 396-cubic-inch engine option, but its power had been toned down to make it more street-friendly. The new powerplant produced only 325 horses. Those who wanted to take their Chevelle to the strip, however, could add a special cam and boost the power to 360 horses.

The 1969 Super Sport had a little-known option for a 427-cubic-inch engine capable of 425 horsepower. Only 358 of these big-block beauties were produced; most of the 1969 Chevelles still carried the 396-cubic-inch engine.

Chevrolet introduced its Chevelle Malibu in 1964 to compete with Ford's Fairlane. Inside, the Chevelle was as roomy as the Impala, but outside it was much smaller, resting on a 115-inch wheelbase.

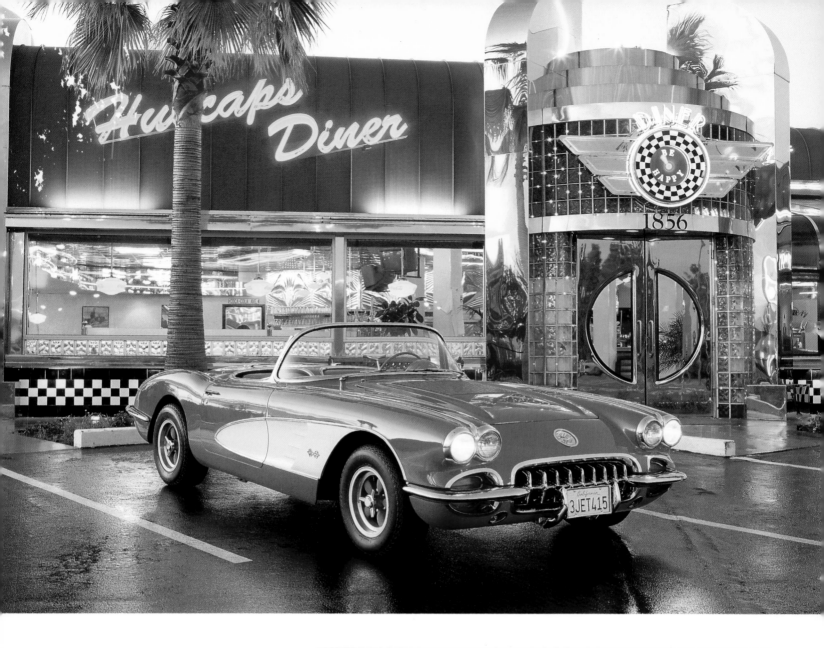

The 1958 fuel-injected Corvette's V-8 engine displaced 283 cubic inches and, depending on options, could produce between 230 and 315 horsepower. It weighed 2,800 pounds, had a wheelbase of 102 inches, an overall length of 177 inches, and sold for a base price of $3,631.

Styling chief for the 1961 Corvette was William L. Mitchell, who gave the car its bobbed ducktail rear. The car still had duel headlamps, but dark mesh now replaced the toothy grille. The 283-cubic-inch V-8 could go from zero-to-sixty in 7.7 seconds.

The Corvette

During the more than forty years since it first appeared in the American showroom, the Corvette has become a cultural icon. It debuted in 1953, the only American-made car of the time to be designed as a high-performance sports car.

The initial version of the car only had a 92-horsepower engine. Considering how light it was, not much more was needed. As the car evolved, of course, the power grew. By 1962, Corvette had a 327-cubic-inch top fuel-injected powerplant (360 horsepower). To keep a handle on all of that performance, the '62 model required a redesigned suspension system and tougher brakes.

With a lighter underlying steel-ladder frame but more steel support structuring than previous models, the 1963 Corvette Sting Ray's 327-cubic-inch engine used a four-barrel carburetor and a solid-lifter camshaft. Its most unusual feature was its split rear window, a design feature of arguable esthetics but dangerously inhibiting to the driver's rear view. The car distributed 2,900 pounds over a 98-inch wheelbase. Twenty thousand '63 Sting Rays were sold at a cost of $4,300 each.

In 1966, the Corvette was powered by the big-block 425-horsepower "Mark

The 1956 Corvette SR-2 convertible had a V-8 engine capable of 265 horsepower. With a wheelbase of 102 inches, and an overall length of 168 inches, it weighed 2,750 pounds. It had a top speed of 120 miles per hour and could go from zero-to-sixty in 7.5 seconds.

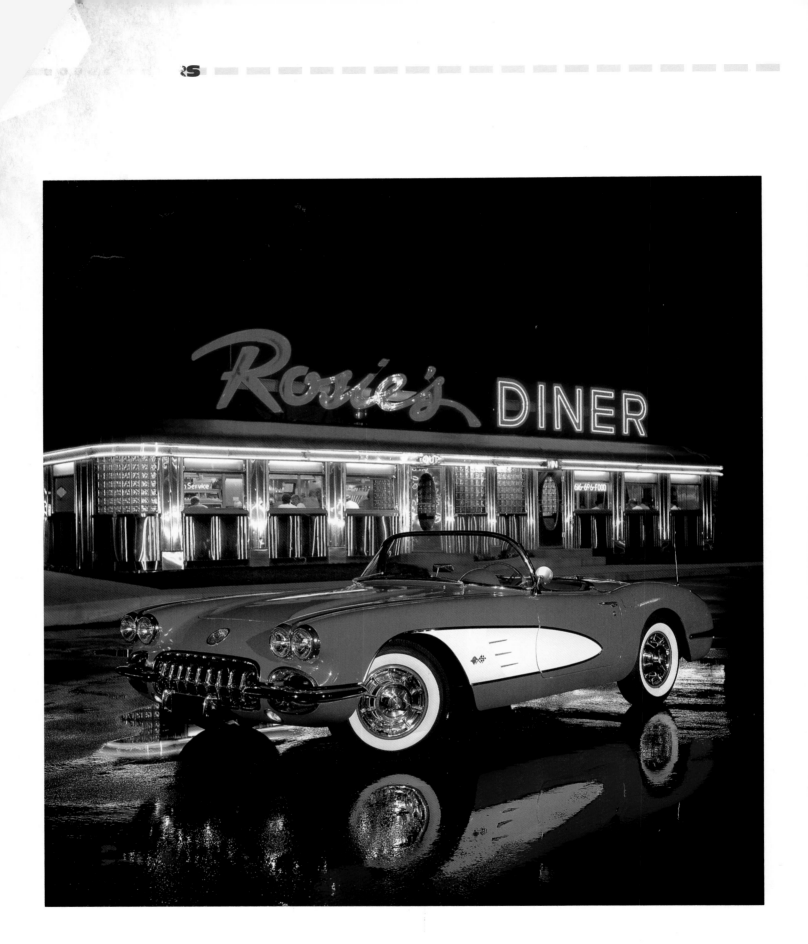

The Corvette debuted in 1953, and by 1960,
when this car was made, it had already
become a national icon. Its lusty youth
epitomized the Detroit Baroque muscle car.

The 1959 Corvette had a camshaft designed by ex-racing driver Zora Arkus Duntov, a Belgian-born Russian who thought the Corvette should be more than just a good-looking car—it should be powerful, too.

The 1966 Corvette 427 had a big-block, 425-horsepower Mark IV engine that could get you from zero-to-sixty in less than 5 seconds. Top speed: 140 miles per hour.

IV" engine. Lucky owners could go zero-to-sixty in less than 5 seconds, with a maximum speed of 140 miles per hour.

The following year, the Corvette Sting Ray debuted the monstrous "L-88" engine: 427 cubic inches and 435 horsepower.

In 1968, Corvettes were built for the first time to comply to federal pollution-control mandates and safety standards. The car was 182.5 inches long with a wheelbase of 98 inches. It weighed 3,100 pounds, and its 327-cubic-inch V-8 engine was capable of only 350 horsepower—down from 435 horses the year before.

The energy and ecological crises that killed other muscle cars only wounded the Corvette. In fact, the 'Vette thrived during the oil shocks and government-mandated downsizing of the 1970s.

The 1963 Corvette Grand Sport had a lighter underlying steel-ladder frame but more steel support structuring than previous models. Its 327-cubic-inch engine used a four-barrel carburetor and a solid-lifter camshaft. The car distri-buted 2,900 pounds over a 98-inch wheelbase.

This 1967 Corvette came with a 427-cubic-inch engine that was as strong as 400 horses.

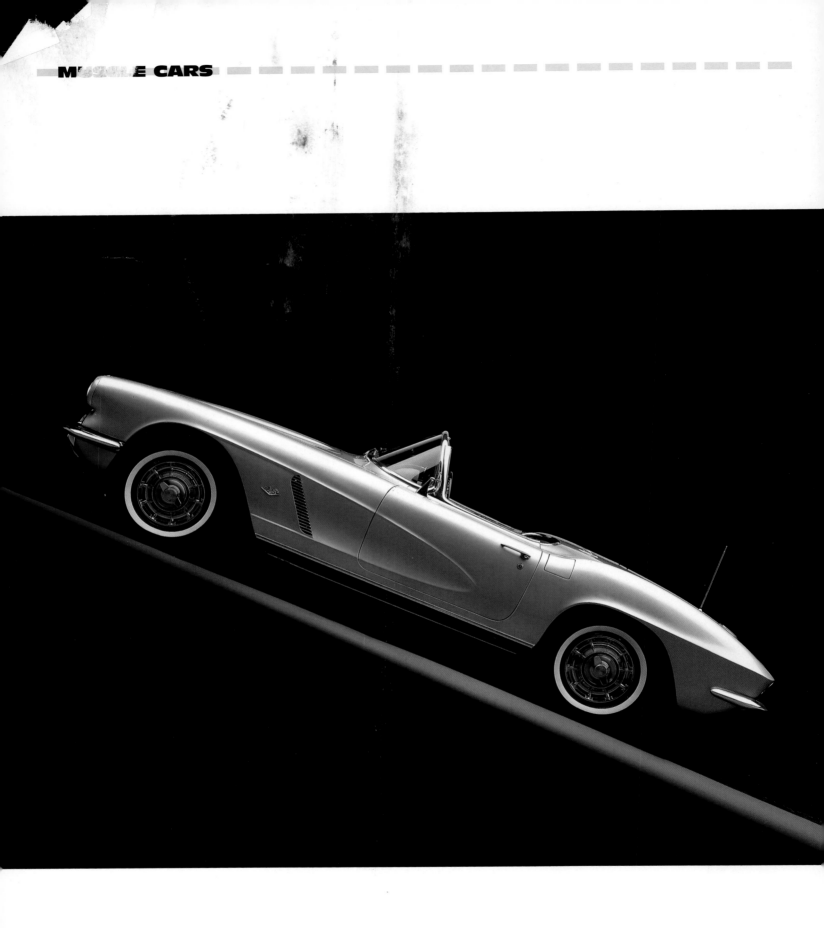

The 1962 Chevrolet Corvette convertible was the first to have the 327-cubic-inch top fuel-injected powerplant (360 horsepower). To keep a handle on all of that performance, there was also a redesigned suspension system and tougher brakes.

Here's the 1974 Stingray Roadster. That was
the year of the first oil embargo, resulting in gas
lines and rationing. The era of cheap, plentiful
gas was through—but the Corvette cruised on!

The combination of race-car designer Carroll Shelby and the new Ford Mustang line spawned this car—the 1966 Shelby GT350—designed to be a race car. When driven on the street, it lacked the comfort of most passenger cars, but it couldn't be beaten at the traffic light.

The Ford Mustang and its Imitators

Originally conceived by the Ford Motor Company as a sporty compact car, the Mustang grew in power and styling until it became Ford's answer to Chevrolet's Corvette. The line made its debut in 1965 with only 164 horses under its hood—but that changed soon enough.

Before long, the Mustang came with enough options to keep everyone happy. There was a perfect version for Mom to use to go to the grocery store, and there was another version for setting pavement afire on the local straightaway.

The 1967 Mustang came with muscles that ranged from putt-putt all the

way to va-*room*. The standard powerplant was a diminutive 200-cubic-incher (115–120 horsepower). Power options topped out with the big block 390-cubic-inch V-8 engine that guzzled gas but responded well to stoplight challenges.

The Mustang became a phenomenally popular car, so naturally it spawned imitators. In the fall of 1966, GM released its response to Ford's Mustang: the 1967 Camaro Super Sport. Its 350-cubic-inch engine, with a 10:1 compression ratio, came standard and was capable of producing 295 horsepower. A few months later, the 396-cubic-inch "L-78" powerplant became optional for the Camaro, muscling up the potential horsepower to 375.

By 1966, when this convertible was produced, the Mustang came with enough options to keep everyone happy. There was a perfect version for Mom to use to go to the grocery store, and there was a consummate version for setting pavement afire on the local straightaway.

The 1967 Pontiac Firebird, after the Chevy Camaro, was General Motors' second attempt to capitalize on the Mustang rage. The 326-cubic-inch engine could crank out as much as 285 horsepower, as long as it was souped up with other options such as dual exhausts and four-barrel carburetion.

In the mid- to late 1960s, Ford cars were winning top honors on all of the racing circuits. Carroll Shelby, the Texas-born Ford car racer and designer, responsible for the Shelby Cobra, became involved in the Mustang project in the mid-1960s; the most notable result was the 1968 Mustang GT-500. This Mustang was considerably larger than any previous version, and that meant that there was plenty of room under the hood for the 428-cubic-inch engine. The powerplant was attached to two four-barrels and could produce 355 horsepower. The GT-500 came with both an automatic transmission and four-speed option.

The 1969 Mustang Mach I was longer, wider, lower, and heavier than previous Mustangs. The standard engine for the Mach I was a 351-cubic-inch V-8 capable of 250 horsepower. Optional were a 390-cubic-inch V-8 producing 320 horsepower; a 428-cubic inch V-8 Cobra Jet with a hood scoop, cranking out 335 horsepower; and a 429-cubic-inch V-8 worth 360 horsepower. Styling included a standard sports-roof fastback, with matte black hood paint, bodyside striping, a special grille with driving lamps, and special wheel trims. The Mach I had a wheelbase of 108 inches and overall length of 187.4 inches; it weighed 3,200 pounds. Prices in 1968 began at $3,139.

Like most muscle cars, the Mustang was still growing as the 1960s came to an end.

FOLLOWING PAGE: The 1964 1/2 Mustang made its public debut at the New York World's Fair, and immediately became tremendously popular—in part because of Ford's time-tested strategy of offering a variety of options packages.

The black interior of the 1968 1/2 Mustang Cobra Jet looked great with the red exterior.

Here's the snazzy snout of the 1968 1/2 Mustang Cobra Jet.

In the fall of 1966, GM released its response to Ford's Mustang: the 1967 Camaro. The car was available both in hard- or ragtop. This 1967 Camaro Street Rod has obviously needed some customization to accommodate its oversized powerplant.

The 1968 Shelby Mustang GT 500—certainly one of the most desirable cars ever made. Standard engine: 428-cubic-inch, 360-horsepower "police interceptor."

The Mustang Boss 429 was—along with the Boss 302 and the Mach 1—one of a team of notable street-fighters produced by Ford in 1969.

The 1969 Pontiac Firebird featured the debut of the "L67 Ram Air IV" package.

The 1969 Camaro SS/RS (left) could be ordered with a huge 427-cubic-inch engine with either an iron or an aluminum block. Both versions were rated at 425 horsepower. Only about a thousand of these special Camaros were produced, and many of them were used for racing. On the right is the version of the 1969 Firebird designated the "Trans Am," which, of course, eventually evolved into its own model.

1969—A Very Good Year

Memories: Cops chasing the 1969 Mercury Cyclone never got to see much but the new dual exhausts; the 427-cubic-inch, 390-horsepower option was still available. . . . The Camaro could be ordered with a humongous 427-cubic-inch engine with either an iron or an aluminum block—both versions were rated at 425 horsepower. Only about a thousand of these special Camaros were produced, and many of them were used for racing.

The Pontiac Firebird featured the debut of the "L67 Ram Air IV" package. One of the versions of the 1969 Firebird was designated the "Trans Am," which, of course, eventually evolved into its own model. . . . Available both as a hardtop and a fast-back, the Ford Fairlane Cobra featured a blacked-out grille, wheel-well moldings, and hood pins; the standard powerplant displaced 428 cubic inches. It was marketed directly toward the young to compete with the Plymouth Road Runner.

The AMC Hurst SC/Rambler was a one-time-only sports car with surprising punch. It was best known for its paint design, which made each one look customized: The standard paint job included a blue arrow that pointed at the hood scoop; on the arrow was written "390 CU. IN.," indicating the number of cubic inches of displacement of the V-8 engine (315 horsepower, 425 foot-pounds of torque).

The 1969 Mercury Cyclone Spoiler looked like a race car that you could drive on the street: Spoilers were running the NASCAR circuit, and no effort was made to disguise that fact on the street machine. Racing mirrors, spoilers both front and back, and a scooped hood looked great, and the Spoiler had a wide variety of optional engines, peaking in power with the 429-cubic-incher, rated at 375 horsepower. On the track, a Cyclone won four NASCAR events in 1969, and it would have won many more if it hadn't been for the clear dominance of its same-factory competitor, the Ford Talladega.

No doubt about it, 1969 was a very good year. But the best was yet to come.

The 1967 Pontiac Firebird Convertible. One of the versions of the 1969 Firebird was designated the "Trans Am," which, of course, eventually evolved 80into its own model.

The 1971 Challenger 440 Six
Pak still had the look, but emis-
sions regulations had hit the
Challenger's performance hard.

CHAPTER TWO

THE 1970s

If asked to name one year that defines the muscle car era, the answer would have to be 1970. Not only did many models peak in power at that time, but there were also more different muscle cars to choose from than ever before—or since.

The 1970 Ford Mustang Boss 302

The 1970 Mustang Boss 302 was a big winner that year on the Trans Am road-racing circuit—and was built with road racing in mind. With a suitably aggressive look, the Boss 302 featured a 302-cubic-inch V-8 worth 290 horsepower. Its styling features included an under-bumper front "chin" spoiler, a trunk-lid wing spoiler, backlight louvers, special side stripes, and a matte black hood. The rare Boss 429 had a Cobra Jet NASCAR engine worth 360 horses. Today, those Boss 429s are ultra-rare collectibles.

The discontinuation, following the 1970 season, of Ford's racing program was a bad sign of things to come for the Mustang line. Still, the 1971 Mustang Mach I could be had with the 429-cubic-inch "Super Cobra Jet" engine. On a drag strip, this car could run the quarter mile in about 13.5 seconds.

The 1970 Dodge Challenger

The Dodge Challenger was a late—almost too late—newcomer to the muscle car scene, making its debut in 1970. Optional engines for the Challenger ranged from the 340-cubic-inch 275-horsepower standard, all the way up to a 425-horsepower Hemi.

The 1970 Ford Mustang Boss 302 was a big winner that year on the Trans Am road-racing circuit—and was built with road racing in mind.

The most elite of the models was the "T/A," designed for the Trans Am racing circuit, though a minimum number of T/As were made for the street to qualify the model for the racing league. The street version had a 340-cubic-inch, three-carburetor engine worth 290 horses; the actual race car, while remaining legally "stock," used an engine with a four-barrel carburetor. The Challenger had heavy-duty shocks, front and rear sway bars, and a rear spoiler.

In 1971, new emissions regulations hit the Challenger hard. Though the model lasted until 1973, it would never be the same.

The 1970 Chrysler 300 Hurst

One of the rarest muscle cars is the 1970 Chrysler 300 Hurst: Only 485 were built. The "Hurst" cars were a joint venture between Chrysler and Hurst Performance products.

Upon receiving a confirmed order for a car, Chrysler would build a white two-door, leaving out the hood, trunk, and interior—but including a 440-cubic-inch engine and other high-performance items. The incomplete car was then shipped to Hurst Performance in Warminster, Pennsylvania, where the Hurst people would finish each one by hand.

The high-performance Hurst package included two-color paint, two-color accent tapes, a fiberglass hood-and-good scoop, "300 Hurst" hood medallions, a fiberglass trunk lid with an incorporated spoiler, a genuine leather interior, a suspension/handling package, disc brakes, a larger radiator, thicker torsion bars, an eight-blade fan, and an AM/FM stereo tape player.

The 1970 Dodge Challenger RT—from that special year when there were more muscle cars to choose from than ever before, or ever after.

In case you're wondering what color this '71 Challenger is, Dodge called it "Plum Crazy."

The 1970 Dodge Challenger RT had to have suspension and drivetrain modifications to accommodate its 383-cubic-inch, 335-horsepower Hemi engine.

There were 16,710 hardtops and 548 convertibles sold of the 1970 Plymouth Barracuda—which was timed on the drag strip with its street-legal engine at 13 seconds for the quarter mile at a speed of 104 miles per hour.

The Plymouths

The Plymouth Superbird was designed specifically for big-time stock-car racing. In 1970, NASCAR rules stated that, in order for a model to qualify for the racing circuit, the manufacturer had to produce at least one car for each dealership. Plymouth built exactly 1903 Superbirds in 1970, and it competed with the Dodge Daytona for the largest wing on a street car.

Superbirds won nine NASCAR races that year with "King" Richard Petty and Pete Hamilton behind the wheel. The Plymouths dominated the circuit that year to such a degree that NASCAR felt obligated to make new rules to equalize the cars—and, in the process, effectively slowed all of them down.

The Plymouth Duster was, like the Road Runner before it, a no-frills muscle car, aimed at the youth market with its ad campaign and affordable price. There were 24,817 Dusters made in 1971, but only half that many the following year.

The Plymouth Barracuda sold 16,710 hardtops and 548 convertibles of the 1970 model—which was timed on the drag strip (with its street-legal engine) at 13 seconds for the quarter mile, at a speed of 104 miles per hour.

The 1970 Plymouth Duster was, like the Road Runner before it, a no-frills muscle car, aimed at the youth market with an ad campaign and an affordable price. There were 24,817 Dusters made in 1971, and about half that many the following year.

Other 1970 Classics

The Mercury Cougar Eliminator looked great with its spoiler in the back and full-length body stripes. Only 2,200 Mercury Cougar Eliminators were constructed in 1970, so anyone who still has one today has a very valuable car. It came with three engine options: a "Boss" 302-cubic-incher (290 horsepower), the 351-cubic-inch "Cleveland," and the big boy, the 428-cubic-inch "Cobra Jet" worth 335 horsepower.

The Pontiac GTO came with an optional 455-cubic-inch powerplant capable of 360 horsepower; a 400-cubic-inch engine was standard. Other options included the Ram Air III and IV engines, rated at 366 and 370 horsepower respectively.

The AMC Rebel Machine was, like the Hurst SC/Rambler, a one-time-only model. Patriotically painted in red, white, and blue, the Rebel Machine had a 390-cubic-inch engine worth 340 horsepower.

The Javelin SST, also from AMC, carried a floor-mounted three-speed shifter. It came in two versions: the Mark Donohue Special (which featured a painted-on logo of the champion race car driver's signature) and the Trans Am.

The Ford Torino GT Cobra, equipped with the new 429-cubic-inch engine, could muster 375 horsepower—perfect for every young American who envisioned a checkered flag at the end of every run.

The Dodge Super Bee came in a color referred to by the factory as "Plum Crazy Purple." Factory options included a remote-controlled left outside mirror, four-speed manual transmission, power steering, rear-window defogger, and a tinted windshield. The powertrain consisted of a 383-cubic-inch Magnum engine with a Hemicrash box four-speed pistol grip.

The Oldsmobile Cutlass came with the famous "W-31" engine. Only 350 cubic inches in displacement, but with power like a rocket, the W-31 made the Cutlass a potential win-

The 1970 Pontiac GTO came with an optional 455-cubic-inch powerplant capable of 360 horsepower. A 400-cubic-inch engine was standard. Other options included the Ram Air III and IV engines, rated at 366 and 370 horse-power respectively.

The 1970 D Super Be options includ a remote-controlled left outside mirro, four-speed manual transmission, power steering, rear-window defogger, and a tinted windshield.

ner on any strip. In 1970, the Cutlass, for the first time, could be driven with the massive 455-cubic-inch "Rochester" four-barrel carburetor engine capable of 365 horsepower.

A one-year wonder, the Oldsmobile Rallye 350 was capable of 310 horsepower, but is best remembered for its look: It came only in yellow with orange and black striping. There were two scoops in the fiberglass hood and a spoiler in the rear.

The Chevrolet Monte Carlo Super Sport was a brand-new model that came with a 454-cubic-inch engine, with options worth 450 horsepower. The Chevelle, like the Super Sport, could be bought with the 454/450 engine, but it was quicker with that power because it was considerably lighter than the Monte Carlo.

The Buick Gran Sport was a heavy car, too (3,562 pounds), but it could be bought with enough muscle under the hood to keep it street-fast. The strongest powerplant option was the 455-cubic-inch engine; it could produce 350 horsepower at 4,600 revolutions per minute. The engine came

The powertrain of the 1970 Dodge Super Bee consisted of a 383-cubic-inch Magnum engine with a Hemicrash box four-speed pistol grip.

The 1970 Buick GSX (Gran Sport Experimental) was only available in two colors: Apollo White or (like this one) Saturn Yellow. The two wide stripes across the hood with their twin scoops made the GSX one of the most easily recognizable models of the year.

with a turbo-400 transmission and a four-barrel quadrajet carburetor. Other factory options included power windows, power bakes, power steering, air conditioning, and tinted glass. A Gran Sport with the 455 engine cost $3,685 in 1970—a little more than a dollar per pound.

The Beginning of the End

It was a two-pronged attack that ended up killing the muscle car. One prong was expensive gas. As the price of gas went up with the "energy crisis" of the early 1970s, most Americans were no longer able to afford the huge quantity of fuel that a muscle car drinks. Driving fast, after all, is a luxury, and when money is short, necessities come first.

The other prong was the environment. The classic muscle cars of the 1960s, as it turned out, were spewing pure poison into the atmosphere. Cities across the nation were choking on auto-produced smog. The first anti-smog law went into effect in California in 1961; it stated that all new cars had to have a system to burn crankcase vapors rather than venting them into the atmosphere.

Buick Skylark 350. The roof is on us.

**Buy a Skylark 350 specially equipped
and we'll give you a sport vinyl top at no charge.**
Buick Bargain Days.
   It means great deals on any new Buick that strikes your fancy.
Take the Skylark 350 Sport Coupe.
If you see your dealer now, order your Skylark with some
   of the options you'd probably want anyway. Like a heavy-duty
   energizer for quick starts. A heavy-duty air cleaner.
   And special instrument gauges and clock.
You'll get the snappy sport vinyl top at no charge.
You'll also be getting a car that traditionally has had the highest
   resale value in its class. And that's saying a lot
   about its value right now.
And since it's a Buick, it's got the features that help make Buicks so easy
   to live with. Like a time-modulated choke for quick starts.
   And a 350-cubic-inch engine that thrives on low-lead or no-lead gas.
   And other good things.

It means it's time to see your Buick dealer.

sail north...

then wheel into the exciting heart of British Columbia!

The MV "Queen of Prince Rupert" is an extension of British Columbia's fine highway system, bridging 330 miles of the fjord-like, coastal Inside Passage. Board with your vehicle at either Prince Rupert or Kelsey Bay on Vancouver Island to complete the Totem Circle tour. Enjoy unparalleled service on this cruise-like ship, then 20 hours later arrive refreshed at your destination to continue your motoring adventure. Drive by the finest native totem poles along the Skeena River. Visit the Cariboo country with its lakes, ranches and goldrush Barkerville, then be awe-struck with the grandeur of the Fraser Canyon. Vancouver and Victoria await you. See your travel agent, auto club, or send for our Totem Circle kit — in any season.

"Camp" along the Inside Passage . . . anytime!

Wheel your recreational vehicle right onto the car deck of the Queen of Prince Rupert. Bring your fishing tackle and camera. British Columbia has something for the outdoors lover all year 'round and there are good camp sites everywhere!

SUMMER (May 8 - Sept. 21) Sailings northbound and southbound on alternate days.
AUTUMN TO SPRING (Sept. 23 - May) Northbound leave Kelsey Bay Tuesdays and Thursdays. Southbound leave Prince Rupert Wednesdays and Saturdays. Off season, save 25% on fares (car, camper, trailer, passenger) and staterooms too! MOTOR COACH connections for all points at both terminals.

BRITISH COLUMBIA FERRIES
Tsawwassen Terminal, Delta, British Columbia

Please send me ferry information

NAME ....

ADDRESS ....

S2E

Salmon River Mountains.

White Water Guest Ranch, Rt. 2, Box 94, Grangeville 83530. Main Salmon River, Salmon River Breaks Primitive Area, and high mountain lakes.

Wilderness Encounters, Inc., Box 274, Idaho Falls 83401. Into Hells Canyon and Seven Devils area.

Southeast Idaho

Vaughn Haderlie, Freedom, Wyo. (on Idaho border) 83120. Caribou and Targhee national forests.

Palisades Creek Ranch, Box 594, Palisades, Idaho 83437. Teton National Forest and Jackson Hole country.

Park's Pack Trip, Box 136, Irwin 83428. Upper Palisades big elk country. Food provided or bring your own.

Twin Lakes Guest Ranch, Box 68, Clifton 83228. Caribou National Forest, Oxford Mountains.

Idaho fly-in trips

Falconberry Looncreek Ranch, 1050 Memorial Dr., Idaho Falls 83401. Twenty-minute flight from Challis. From lodge into heart of Idaho Primitive Area.

Flying 'R' Outfitters, Rt. 1, Box 94D, Kamiah 83536. From base camp reached by plane from Grangeville, trips into Selway River and Moose Creek in Selway-Bitterroot Wilderness. Everything furnished or handle own food and cooking.

Flying W Ranch, Rt. 2, Box 242, Emmett 83617. Take plane from Emmett. Idaho Primitive Area.

MacKay Bar's Stonebreaker Ranch, Box 1099, Boise 83701. An hour from Boise. From Chamberlain Basin into nearby lakes in Idaho Primitive Area.

Peck's Ponderosa, Box 493H, Challis 83226. Take plane from Challis. Into middle fork of Salmon River, and Big Horn Crags.

Sleeping Deer Ranch, Box 212, Challis 83226. Fly in from Challis or pack in. From ranch into drainage area of Salmon River's middle fork.

Idaho trips with access by jet boat

Idaho Vacations, Inc., Box 204, Eagle 83616. Reached by 20-mile jet boat from Riggins. Salmon River area around Warren and gold mining towns.

Nez Perce Outfitters & Guides, Box 1454, Salmon 83467. Reached by jet boat. Into Salmon River Breaks, Idaho Primitive Area, Big Horn Crags.

White Water Boatman, Box 705, Salmon 83467. High lake country of Salmon River Breaks Primitive Area. Trip ends with jet boat ride to base camp.

By 1963 the California regulation had become national. In 1966, a new California law stated that new-car hydrocarbon emissions had to be less than 275 parts per million and less than 1.5 percent carbon monoxide. More new regulations—most notably the Clean Air Act—followed periodically, especially after the Environmental Protection Agency was established in 1970. The cost of all this to the muscle car lover was horsepower!

Diminishing Strength

Muscle car power numbers peaked in 1970. Most models began to downsize. "Gas mileage" became an issue for the first time. Economical foreign compact cars became a larger threat to Detroit than ever before. Those American models that kept their big block engines founds sales shrinking. Mostly, however, the thing that was shrinking was the displacement of the powerplants.

The 1971 Pontiac Firebird Trans Am debuted the new 455-cubic-inch engine, but only 2,116 were sold. Only 124 of the 1971 Buick GSXs were built. It would be the last year that the GSX would be available, with its 455-cubic-inch standard engine capable of 345 horsepower. The 1971 Dodge Challenger was the last of the line to offer the Hemi-engine option.

The Death of the GTO

The 1971 Pontiac GTO looked every bit as good as the 1970 model, but the line's performance had peaked. The 455-cubic-inch engine was now rated at 325 horsepower, down from 360 the previous year. The GTO would never be the same. The 1972 GTO continued the downward slide; its engine was now capable of only 300 horsepower.

The 1973 LeMans GTO was a mere shadow of earlier GTOs. Once capable of 455 horses, the most powerful option available under the hood in 1973 offered only 250 horsepower. The next year that was down to 200 horsepower, at which point the series was mercifully put to rest.

Last Gasps

The 1972 Chevy Chevelle had 350-cubic-inch/175-horsepower, 396-cubic-inch/240- horsepower, and 454-cubic-inch/270-horsepower engine options. The top engine available for the 1973 Dodge Charger was a 340-cubic-inch "Magnum"; emissions laws had rendered the 426 Hemi and 440 Six Pack a thing of the past. The 1972 Dodge Demon's power was hurt by new compression-ratio reduction rules, and its best horsepower rating was reduced to 240. And by 1973, the Plymouth Barracuda still had the look of a muscle car, but—like much of the Detroit product—it had been robbed of its strength.

FOLLOWING PAGE: You didn't need a fortuneteller to know that the 1970 Oldsmobile Cutlass 4-4-2 could tear up the blacktop!

The Chevelle had already started its downward slide in 1971, as the muscle-car era came to an end.

One exception to the shrinking-power rule of the 1970s was the 1974 Dodge Dart Sport, which had a 360-cubic-inch powerplant with a two-barrel carburetor, worth 245 horsepower. In a time when engines were getting smaller and weaker, this model's engine grew larger and stronger from the previous year.

The 1973 Pontiac Trans Am represented another of the last gasps of the muscle car era. The engine was called the "LS2 455 Super Duty." Its 455 cubic inches of displacement could get 290 horses right out of the factory, and 375 horses when souped up for the racetrack. The engine came with high-flow cylinder heads, a Quadrajet carburetor, four-bolt mains, and forged pistons and rods.

The 1974 Pontiac Firebird with the "SD-455" engine (455 cubic inches) produced 290 horsepower. It was definitely a sign of the times that no street engine produced in the United States that year was stronger.

*The 1971 Dodge Charger
R/T earned fame on the
TV show* Dukes of Hazard.

*The engine of the famous 1971
Dodge Charger R/T, which
got more screen mileage than
any other car during the 1970s.*

The big-block 1968 Chevrolet Camaro Z-28 had new multileaf springs, a tilting steering wheel, tinted glass, a redesigned dashboard (including a factory-mounted tachometer), a new grille, staggered shocks, and changes in the suspension. In 1968, 184,178 V-8-powered Camaros were produced. Of these, 40,977 came with the Rally Sport option, 27,884 with the SS option, and 7,199 with the Z option. When the 1968 Camaro first appeared, its price ranged from $2,638 to $2,941.

CHAPTER THREE

RESTORING MUSCLE CARS

Since, for the most part, American car manufacturers are no longer making muscle cars in their factories, it is up to the independent mechanics of this country to find muscle cars from years past and to restore them to their original beauty and power. Here are some stories of dedicated car restorers and their labors of love.

The 1972 Oldsmobile Cutlass

George Randolph of Utica, New York is a civil engineer who enjoys restoring muscle cars in his spare time. His first project, back in the 1980s, was the frame-up restoration of a 1972 Oldsmobile Cutlass. He had no idea what he was getting into: The restoration ended up taking him four years to complete.

"When the '72 Olds Cutlass first came out no one thought of it as a muscle car," Randolph explains. "A boat, yes—but not necessarily prime muscle." Today however, in retrospect, one only has to look at the sleek body styling and the 310 horses produced by its 455-cubic-inch engine to see that this was a bona fide member of the muscle car era.

"My Cutlass feeds its 455 engine into a turbo 400 transmission, then a 3.73:1 rear end. This gear range, in the upper threes, produces a machine that is fast, but still manageable on the street," says Randolph. "The trans has a dual gate shifter."

Other stock items remaining on Randolph's Cutlass include the outside temperature gauge, Rallye steering wheel, interior, and SSII sport wheels. The car has been carefully painted in white and brown, preserving the hood accents that were used at the time.

"The paintwork took up most of the time," says Randolph, "but I also put a lot of effort into detailing the engine with an aluminum manifold, Holley carburetor, chrome air cleaner, and some other stuff." The engine, however, is basically stock—aside from those few high-performance modifications.

History has proven that the 1972 Oldsmobile Cutlass was a muscle machine with high-performance horsepower. It had a size and body style comparable to large luxury cars. This combination means the '72 Cutlass remains popular among those who like a big, comfortable car with excellent response to the gas pedal.

The 1968 Chevrolet Camaro Z-28 Rally Sport

There were only 7,199 Z-28s made in 1968, so John Gardner of Green Bay, Wisconsin searched for years for one before he struck paydirt. He bought his '68 Camaro Z-28 from a farmer in Kenosha, Wisconsin, and was pleased to find that the car was so close to perfect that very little restoration work was necessary.

The original factory options that remain on the car include the power front disc brakes, Rally sport package, console gauge package, and tachometer. The paint job is stock LeMans blue with black stripes, and the black interior remains one hundred percent stock original.

The cockpit of the most performance-oriented Camaro of them all: the 1968 Z-28. Its 302-cubic-inch engine could produce 295 horses.

"The engine has been modified for better performance," says Gardner. "The 302-cubic-inch V-8 produces 290 horsepower, which is fed through a four-speed manual 'M-21' transmission to a twelve-bolt General Motors positraction rear end."

The engine components that have been added include new valve heads, a mechanical lifter camshaft, and Harland Sharp roller rocker arms. It has the stock Z-28 manifold and a Holley four-barrel carburetor.

The 1968 Camaro was a small, lighter muscle car with a big engine, patterned after Ford's Mustang. But the Camaro is not just a copy of another manufacturer's car: It has a distinctive body style and handling features that have made it a favorite among many muscle car restorers.

The 1977 Chevrolet Corvette

Slip on in and ride! Jonathan Cummings of Akron, Ohio, a sales representative, is the owner of a 1977 'Vette that has been carefully restored to its original condition with as few after-market replacement parts and modifications as possible.

He spent years searching for a stock Corvette that was in excellent condition—until he finally found what he was looking for. "I purchased the car as is, cleaned it up, and added a few needed parts. In fact, the Mickey Thompson chrome valve covers on the 210-horsepower Chevy 350 engine are the only parts that are not stock," says Cummings.

The car was originally purchased with just about all of the available factory options: air conditioning, automatic transmission, etc. Since buying the car, Cummings has sanded and repainted the inside of the hood, cleaned the engine compartment, replaced the carpeting, installed new brakes, rebuilt the carburetor, added new Eagle GT Tires, and made other cosmetic improvements.

The 1979 Pontiac Trans Am

Charlie Tusk's '79 Trans Am has 150,000 miles on it—but it sure doesn't look it. Tusk, a mechanic from Lincoln, Nebraska, has put a lot of restoration work into his beauty during the ten years since he bought it.

"It was driven every day for two years during the period just before restoration began," Tusk explains. "When I first got the car, in 1986, I began replacing parts one by one. Soon, it got to the point where I couldn't stand the sight of old parts next to new ones."

To solve the problem, he began to re-do the entire car. "She still has her original upholstery, which is in superb condition. Otherwise, just about everything is new," Tusk says. "The nice thing about having a '79 Trans Am is that most of the factory parts are still available." (You might want to keep that in mind for your own car restoration project: late-period muscle cars' parts are often easier to acquire. The way time passes, it will be a collectors' item before long anyway.)

Tusk describes how he went about restoring his car: "Before painting it, I did the body work. The original paint was GM silver, which I kept. I used a PPG Ditzler Deltron basecoat, topped off with a clear coat. The stock engine, the big 403 Olds, was kept but was detailed to give it a restored look. Detailing included braided lines, polished parts—and repainting where necessary.

"I replaced the interior carpeting and the air conditioning was removed to provide better access to the engine—but otherwise, it is stock."

None of the original options were changed. Those included power seats, brakes, and windows. Tusk's Pontiac will no doubt become more valuable with each passing year.

The 1968 Camero SS396 came with metallic brake linings, power disks, power brake booster, power steering, high-ratio manual steering, and an assortment of rear-axle ratios.

The 1969 Plymouth Barracuda 440 FB received a facelift after 1968, making it look more than ever like a Mustang.

The 1965 Dodge Coronet RT Convertible

Any way you look at it, the restoration of a 1965 Dodge Coronet RT convertible by Robert Flannagan of Kansas City, Missouri is quite a rarity! The '68 Coronet is an unusual car, in that it combines a lot of body, engine, and interior restoration work with some fine work on the Dodge powerplant. The engine is a 383 with 440 heads; with the factory four-speed, the car can muster an estimated 400 horsepower.

Flannagan got the car by trading a Chevy pickup, along with a promise to restore the Dodge. "When I got it, the engine had already been modified," says Flannagan. "That includes the chrome valve covers, air cleaner, flex fan, Mallory dual-point distributor, Accel coil, and Hedman headers."

Flannagan owns an auto shop in Kansas City, so he gutted and rebuilt his Coronet there. "I took out a lot of bondo from the rear quarters and bottom front fenders," Flannagan explains. "I wire-brushed the entire body until I got down to the metal, and then I put on three coats of Duro extend to fill in the pit marks. Six months later, the body was sanded and the metal work was done."

Flannagan then installed the seats and door panels, and added new black cloth headliners, black velour seats with red suede inserts, and red carpeting.

"I then restored the dashboard to factory specifications with the addition of a 3-inch tachometer by Sun," Flannagan says. "The tachometer was placed in a hole originally made for the clock, so no new holes needed to be cut into the dashboard."

In addition to all of that work, Flannagan also installed all-new front-end parts, near rear springs, and an electric fuel pump. "I also rebuilt all of the brakes," he adds.

Now the Kansas City mechanic would like to know how many 1965 Coronet 440s are out there. "I have never seen another Coronet 440 with a factory four-speed," he admits.

The 1969 Plymouth Barracuda

Jim McLernon, a Phoenix, Arizona art director, has customized and restored his 1969 Barracuda into a quick street machine. The 340-cubic-inch engine, attached to a four-speed transmission, has been completely rebuilt to high-performance specifications.

"This involved boring the block .030 over, rebuilding the heads, and installing a Hemi grind camshaft and a Predator carburetor," comments McLernon. "It also has a new rear end, new driveshaft, and the drivetrain has also been completely rebuilt."

The Barracuda's exterior has been painted with a jet black acrylic enamel, a fire- red stripe, and then covered with a clear coat. The interior was re-done using red and black crushed velour. New carpeting was added.

"Parts that have been replaced include the rear differential, brakes, lines, tires, wheels, shocks, suspension, and most engine accessories. Everything but the water pump and windshield washer motor are new," says McLernon.

The 1966 Chevrolet Chevelle SS Two-Door Hardtop

Bill Dudley of Addison, Illinois—a member of Chicago's Classic Chevy Cruisers Club—has done wonders with his '66 Chevy Chevelle. He has beautifully restored the body and the interior, and the high-performance engine has been heavily modified.

"The engine has been completely rebuilt," Dudley explains. "I bought the Chevelle just after I graduated from high school. I learned everything I know from my dad who

The 1969 Plymouth Barracuda 440 FB came with the largest engine available in a Barracuda.

The nifty barracuda remained next to the taillight on the 1969 Plymouth Barracu

also restores cars." His Chevelle's 396-cubic-inch engine has been bored .030 over. "It has a three-angle valve job, ported and polished heads, ten-to-one compression, headers, a Mallory ignition system, and a Holley 750 carburetor," Dudley says.

"My Chevelle's accessories include original Mickey Thompson valve covers, braided lines, and a chromed master cylinder. The body is painted 'Cadillac gunmetal gray' with a pearl clear coat, all lacquer. The interior is painted gloss metal black. The upholstery is gray velour with black vinyl. It has black carpeting and a black vinyl headliner." The louvered inserts on the hood are an interesting original body feature.

The 1971 Ford Mustang Mach I

Although the 1971 Ford Mustang Mach I could be purchased with the 429-cubic-inch "Super Cobra Jet" engine, Stacy Thompson of Denver, Colorado owns one with the 351-cubic-inch, 285 horsepower engine. His Mach I, however, has a host of rare factory options that have been kept intact.

"I bought the car nine years ago from a vintage car dealer," Thompson says. "It had already received a lot of work when I got it and it was in excellent condition. But it was no longer stock. I wanted to change it back so that it could be stock again. So, piece by piece, I returned it to the exact way it was when it was new."

The original factory options included the Mach I package, staggered rear shock absorbers, a deluxe interior, a rear window defroster, electric windows, tilt steering wheel, rear fold-down seat, Magnum wheels, front and rear spoilers, and a three-spoke rim-blown steering wheel.

"I had to repaint the hood, put it back to Mach I black," Thompson says. "I also removed a chrome bumper and installed a urethane original bumper." Thompson also installed a 1971 spread-bore intake and carburetor, and changed the distributor back to a 1971 factory dual point. The hoses, belts, filters, and battery were changed back to factory.

"The only other parts that are not original are the shifter and the seat belts," Thompson says. That's because he has installed the preferred Hurst package for those.

The 1986 Ford Mustang GT

Betty and Barney Bloom of Bradford, Pennsylvania have souped up their '86 Mustang so effectively that it is now lightning quick. The Blooms have taken their car to the local quarter-mile track just to see what it can do—and even they were slightly stunned when the machine performed to the tune of 12.75 seconds at 112.8 miles per hour!

What makes those numbers even more impressive is the care the Blooms have taken to keep their Mustang completely emissions- and street-legal. The car still has its catalytic converters, stock power steering, and air pump fully operational.

"She runs great now, but we got off to a real bad start with her," says Betty. "We added nitrous oxide when we first got it," adds Barney. "Immediately blew a gasket in the stock 302-cubic-inch engine." "While we had the engine apart, we decided to do it right and make a fast, street-legal GT," Betty sums up.

"We rebuilt the engine using high-performance add-on components," says Barney. "I replaced the stock camshaft with a Kaufman Products Stage III cam kit. That included a billet roller camshaft, double valve springs, and roller rockers." Other high-performance modifications include nitrous oxide by NOS and Mickey Thompson I Series rear tires.

The stock 1986 shrouded valve heads were removed and replaced with early casting (1977–1985) non-shrouded heads with stainless steel valves with a three-angle valve job. He also added a set of under-drive pulleys.

The aluminum water pump, alternator, air pump, balancer, and brackets have been painted Ford gray. The stock headers were painted aluminum, and the valve covers have been polished to give the engine a customized look. The hoses have been covered with stainless-steel covers and clamp covers.

The Mustang's body is all stock except for the GTS headlight covers and SVO rear wing and Ford mud flaps. Inside, the car has a Hurst shifter, pull-out AM/FM cassette tape player, and a Pioneer 60-watt amplifier.

All told, this car is capable of 400 horsepower—proving that, with the right parts and expertise, a mid-1980s car *can* be a muscle car.

Whitewall tires and fins were two of the elements that gave the '57 Chrysler 300C convertible its great look.

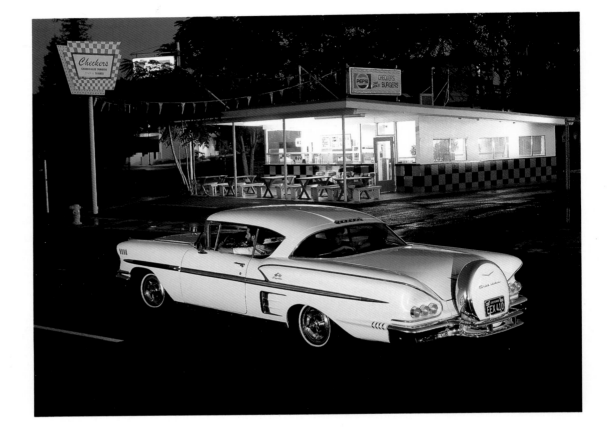

...ions ...red an ...of the 1960s, ...America's love affair with the automobile started in the 1950s, mostly because of the incredibly beautiful designs—such as that on the 1958 Chevrolet Impala Sport Coupe.

The 1963 Ford Custom 300 was built during Ford's heyday in motorsports.

Th[...]
Im[...]a[...]
could be [...]e[...]
a 409-cub[...]-inc[...]
plant capable of [...]
horses. To help c[...]ntro[...]
all that power, the
Impala had heavy-
duty shocks, stiffer
springs, and sintered
metal brake linings.

Optional engines for
the 1966 Dodge Charger
(its debut year), included
the 426-cubic-inch Hemi
engine. Known for its
extended fastback, the
back bucket seats folded
down so that it could
haul things just like a
station wagon. Not that
this was a family vehi-
cle—the speedometer
went to 150 miles per
hour and the tachometer
could measure 6,000
revolutions per minute.

The 1966 Plymouth
Belvedere Satellite, the
car that Richard Petty
drove to the NASCAR
championship.

Like Shelby's Cobra, the 1965 Ford Shelby GT350 was built on an individual basis, and almost all of the 562 units produced of this car were unique.

The 1966 Chevy Malibu had the engine of a muscle car but the body of a ninety-eight pound weakling. It had power, all right, but it suffered from mediocre handling and provided a noisy ride.

The 1968 Mercury
Cyclone GT featured
an automatic trans-
mission that made
it a comfy cruiser,
but a lousy racer.
On the strip, she
tended to shift at
the wrong times.

This 1967 Oldsmobile
Cutlass convertible.
This isn't your . . .
well, yes, this is your
father's Oldsmobile.

The 1969 Chevy Camaro was available
in more different guises than any other
car produced that year—and the Chevrolet
marketing department was there for
them all. Among the models available
was the SS, which could really fly.

The 1968 Ford GT-40 earned world-
wide attention by giving Ferrari
a run for their money at the 24-
Hours of Le Mans endurance race.

The '67 Dodge Roadster Daroo was an odd-looking duck. From some angles it is difficult to tell the front from the back. From others, it looked more like a boat than a car. But from behind the wheel, the view was beautiful—a little blurry, but beautiful.

The ZL-1 model of the 1969 Chevy Camaro— obviously an extremely patriotic purchase!

The Camero RS Z-28 was a package that grew quickly in popularity. When it was introduced in 1967, it only sold 600 units. That number went up to 7,199 in 1968. By 1969, the year that this car was produced, 19,000 Z-28s would be sold.

The 1969 Oldsmobile 4-4-2, like most muscle cars, had its weak point in the braking system. These cars were meant to go, not stop.

The 1968 Oldsmobile 4-4-2, which competed in the marketplace against cars such as the Road Runner, Mustang Cobra, AMX, and Pontiac GTO.

The 1970 Chevy Nova was too heavy to satisfy power-freaks, and most units were purchased by families.

The 1969 Dodge Dart Swinger got 275-horsepower from its 340-cubic-inch engine.

The 1969 Plymouth GTX was designed as a straightforward high-performance car, which came with an option for a 426-cubic-inch Hemi engine.

AFTERWORD

By the mid-1970s the muscle car era was fully dead. Can it ever return? Like innocence, the era would be difficult to recapture. But before we say that muscle cars are gone forever, there is reason for optimism.

Americans are buying bigger cars (and trucks) and driving them at faster speeds than they have in a generation. The reason: lower gasoline prices. The oil cartel that caused the rapid rise in gas prices during the early 1970s is broken. Adjusted for inflation, gas prices are lower right now than they have been at any time since the 1950s. The American Petroleum Institute says that consumption of gasoline in the United States rose 1.1 percent in 1992, 1.4 percent in 1993, 1.7 percent in 1994, and a whopping 2.5 percent in 1995. More and more, conversations about "what she can do" have replaced those about "how much does she get."

It is also meaningful that, according to the New York State Police, the average speeding ticket in 1994 went to a driver going 73 miles per hour. In 1995, that figure went up to 76 miles per hour.

And let's not forget that there are only four states in the nation—Connecticut, Hawaii, New Jersey, and Rhode Island—that still have a 55-mile-per-hour speed limit everywhere. The era of conservation and restraint is over.

The 1996 Dodge Viper GTS Coupe has an eight-liter, 450-horsepower, aluminum V-10 engine. The 1996 Chevrolet Camaro Z28 SS can get 310 horsepower with its 350-cubic-inch engine plus an optional exhaust upgrade. Corvettes, of course, still have numbers just as impressive, at a heftier price.

How long can it be before Detroit decides to take advantage of a rekindled muscle car market?

You could still get the 426-cubic-inch engine cam which necessitated structural reinforcement in the 1974 Plymouth Road Runner, but it had been four years since the line stopped carrying the Hemi option.

The 1968 Dodge Charger R/T was a semi-fastback with a four-barrel, 440-cubic-inch engine, capable of 375 horsepower. It weighed a hefty 4,400 pounds and some drivers complained that it lacked cornering stability.

INDEX

Page numbers in **bold-face** type indicate photo captions.

Ray Manley's

HOPI KACHINAS

Text by Clara Lee Tanner

RAY MANLEY PUBLISHING
238 SOUTH TUCSON BLVD.
TUCSON, ARIZONA 85716

Ray Manley's: HOPI KACHINAS

Hopi Indians have lived for centuries in a relatively barren and dry part of the great Plateau country of northern Arizona. Here they have established a rapport with nature which has sustained them through many disasters such as droughts and crop failures. Here they have developed a philosophy in response to all about them, to sunshine and snow, to rain and blowing sands, to plants which have nourished them or which held disaster in their dark green leaves, to animals large and small, and to their own kind in a closely knit social order. This philosophy is expressed in their religion which links all in a great oneness, in a great balance, in a reciprocal system of high order.

Additional concepts evolved through the long and tedious years to eventuate in a belief by the Hopis that pairing is to be found in all things. Plants, animals, all aspects of nature, man—all have a dualism reflected in two forces, the visible and the spirit counterpart. "Kachinas are the spirit essence of everything in the real world," says Barton Wright in his 1977 publication, HOPI KACHINAS, *The Complete Guide to Collecting Kachina Dolls.* This is but one aspect of the kachina cult, it is but one facet of the complex Hopi religion.

And what is a kachina? A definitive answer, a complete answer cannot be given. As used by the Hopis it includes, among other things, the spirits of the ancestors, clouds, deities, intermediaries between man and the gods. Too, in a sense, kachina is the steam which rises from hot food, the vapor which water emits on a cold morning. These things are the kachina spirits, they are the kachinas themselves. All of the kachinas live half the year on the tops of great mountains near the Hopi mesas such as the San Francisco Peaks. During the other half of the year they live on the Hopi mesas.

On specific occasions Hopi men dress and mask to personate these spirits; virtually the spirits become part of them, and they *are* the kachinas at such times. Power and spirit are vested in the dancer's masks too, so much so, in fact, that certain major types must be kept out of sight of all when not in use. Then there are kachina dolls, the carved, painted, and bedecked figures which duplicate the dancer, his mask, his costume, body paint, and the paraphernalia which he carries. Flat kachina dolls, called cradle dolls, are given to baby boys and girls to protect them in infancy, while regular kachina dolls are given to girls, and rarely, to older Hopi women.

Evidently kachinas were part of the religious beliefs of the prehistoric ancestors of the Hopi Indians and have continued to be significant among these tribesmen to the present moment. Evidences for their antiquity include masked figures painted on pottery and on the walls of their ceremonial chambers called kivas, plus occasional carved figures found in prehistoric sites. Some of the painted figures, and particularly their masks, are so like contemporary ones that they can be named. One carved and painted wooden figurine found in a cave near Phoenix measures 7¼" in height. It is so like early historic dolls, and those of some Rio Grande villages today, in its mask, its absence of limbs, its simple rounded body, that it is often referred to as a kachina doll.

Historically, the first known kachina dolls were obtained in 1857. From then on others were picked up sporadically until about the end of the 19th century. Little is known about these except that they were basically simple in style, with slightly detailed masks and quite simplified bodies. Much more comes to light as a result of the great photographers, such as A. C. Vroman, at the turn of the century. Some of these men have left records of actual dolls hanging on the walls of Hopi homes or in collections. Amazingly, at this early time there are large and small carved kachinas, there are both static and dynamic styles, there are figures with little or no form and some with fair form in body, arms, and legs. Both styles continue to the present, with development of the modelled and free-form action dolls in recent years.

Kachina doll making today involves both tradition and creativity. Although they have tried other materials, the Hopi Indian still prefers and uses drift cottonwood root. Formerly available in washes close to their villages or from the Grand Canyon area, today the doll maker most frequently purchases a ready-cut piece of a certain length, usually at a high price. Tools are adapted to remove bark, to smooth the wood, to form and finish the piece, and often to make any necessary additional parts, such as head pieces, or a tiny rattle or bow, or various body parts.

These tools include hand saws, mallets, hatchets, hammers, chisels, rasps, and knives, the last from pocket to butcher styles.

Formerly the doll was made as a single piece, particularly the simpler ones. Some of those with large headpieces or great ears had these carved as separate pieces, then they were attached to the doll. Today arms, legs, headpiece, and sometimes even the head itself may all be carved separately and then joined to the body. Despite the elaborate nature of some of the latter, the doll made from a single piece of wood is still favored above all others by some collectors.

After the doll is completely carved and assembled, it is given an all-over whitewash, usually with native kaolin clay, although modern substitutes may be used. Then follows the detailed painting, formerly with native mineral or vegetal dyes, later with water colors or tempera (poster paints long a favorite), and today with modern acrylics, this last a superior medium in all respects. Paints were applied in earlier years and for quite some time thereafter with yucca brushes; today any brush may be used, including some of sable.

Last are added various items, unless they have been carved with the rest of the doll. A ruff about the neck was formerly made of green-bough, this followed by substitute materials such as plastics, and with yarns a favored material today. Objects placed in the hands are carefully made, such as rattles, bows, and knives. Jewelry may be painted on the doll, or tin and blue commercial beads may substitute for silver and turquoise. Today the latter two, plus shells from all over the world are not uncommonly used on better dolls. Necklaces, bow guards, earrings, and bracelets are made of these materials. Clothing runs the gamut from carved and painted semblances on the wood to actual pieces of cloth with proper decoration on each garment. Fur from small native animals have long been favored for ruffs about the neck and for hair or as worn pendant from the waist at the back; today these may be replaced by commercial fur. Formerly colored feathers from specific birds were used to decorate the headpieces of specific kachinas; today feathers come from domestic fowl or sparrows—or are carved.

Masks are the most important part of the doll, as is true in the kachina which it represents, for this feature truly identifies the original personage. In earlier dolls, or even in more poorly executed ones today, the body paint, dress, and other details may be neglected. However, in the better doll today some or all of these features are exquisitely executed, as is illustrated in many kachinas in this publication. For instance, embroidery and brocade designs on men's kilts and sashes may be duplicated from the original, as are the wide black (or dark blue) and red bands on the woman's shoulder blanket. Fur ruffs about the neck may be real or carved. Body paint is often indicative of a specific kachina, such as the large rounds of white on a black background on the lower arms and legs of Mountain Lion and Wolf.

Certain Hopi customs are reflected in some kachina details; so too are some of their legends or myths. When young girls are ready for marriage their hair is done up in two great whorls, one at each side of the head, as represented in many "Kachin Manas" or female kachinas. However, on Warrior Maiden there is one whorl only, with the hair at the other side of the head hanging loose. The story goes that in the long ago this maid was dressing when the enemy suddenly appeared. Although her hair was but half done, she picked up her father's weapons and successfully defended her village.

In the modern doll, anatomy is frequently well presented, which is another great advance in carving. In the currently well-made pieces not only is there modelling in form but also a show of muscles, in both features in the body proper as well as in arms and legs, all of this producing a more realistic figure. A few carvers have exaggerated these features to the point of the grotesque. Further, pieces are often today referred to as action dolls, for the artist presents the body, arms and legs in positions of motion in the dance. It is in the beautifully modelled action doll that some Hopi carvers have crossed over from the crafts into the realm of the fine arts.

Objects appearing in the hands of the kachina, and in its doll counterpart, often indicate to some degree what he does or who he is. For example, these items might include bows, rattles, sticks, staffs, yucca whips, or even a sword-like affair, a saw, or a butcher knife. Yucca

whips are appropriately carried by the Whipper Kachinas, to be used to strike blows on the young initiates and on each other during the proper ceremony. Or such whips may also be in the hands of some of the Guard Kachinas, to be used, if necessary, to keep crowds from moving in too close to a ceremony. One or two sticks will be carried in the hands of Deer, Antelope, and some other Animal Kachinas to represent their front legs. Disciplinary Ogre Kachinas are frequently equipped with all too realistic butcher knives or saws, bows and clubs to frighten the children, or they carry baskets on their backs into which they might threaten to throw a naughty child.

Two basic concepts have been influential in the development of the kachina cult and the ceremonies in which kachinas have become an active part, namely, fertility and the need for moisture. Like most simple agricultural societies the world over, these two needs became so vital that they were incorporated into specific ceremonies. Thus did tribesmen seek supernatural aid to attain their desired ends, water and successful crops.

Perhaps as the result of hundreds of years of trial and error, of experimentation and contemplation, the Hopis eventually worked out an annual cycle or "calendar" of religious events fundamentally related to these two needs. Timing of ceremonies was based on the positions of the sun and moon in relation to natural objects, such as a mesa edge or mountain peak. Basically, one half of the year is concerned with kachina or masked dances, these held from December to

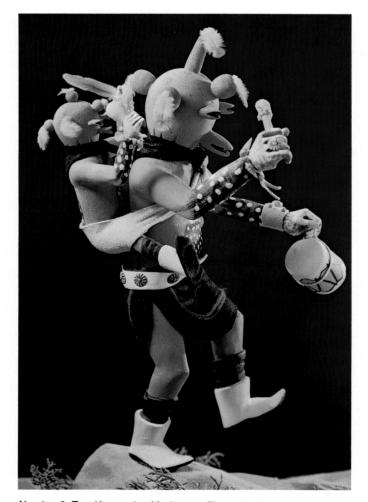

Number 2: Two Koyemsi or Mudheads. These kachinas appear in most of the Hopi dances in multiple roles. Sometimes they are drummers, or they announce dances, or they just "clown around" to entertain, or play games with the people who have gathered to watch the performances.

July, and the other half of the year with non-masked ceremonies which are presented from July into December.

Among the important summer rites, with no masked dancers, are the Flute and Snake ceremonies, both concerned with water. The lovely Flute Dance, held by villages in years alternating with the Snake Ceremony, is performed in part at springs on the edges of the Hopi mesas, basically to insure the continuation of this source of water. Lenang, the Flute Kachina, must not be confused with this rite; he does not appear at this time, but rather, in the regular Kachina season. More important from the standpoint of figures carved by Hopis is the Snake Dance, an August ritual for rain and crop maturation. The unmasked Snake Dancer (see page 14) is frequently produced by kachina carvers, and has been since the turn of the century. As unmasked personages, these dancers are not kachinas. Other important dances of this non-kachina season include Women's Society Dances, and important initiation ceremonies.

There are other unmasked performers favored by carvers. Some, like Butterfly and Buffalo, perform in Social Dances rather than in the kachina rituals. Oddly, some carvers often embellish Butterfly Dancer with a mask, despite the fact that as she performs she merely has bangs of hair hanging over her eyes. The real Butterfly Girl, known as Poli Mana, is not masked, although she is often represented with a mask by carvers in their dolls. She is often confused with Palhik' Mana, Water Drinking Girl or also Butterfly Girl, who appears on Third Mesa as a masked dancer during Kachina season. Both Butterfly dolls, whether the real Butterfly Girl or the Butterfly Kachina Girl, are among the loveliest of all carvings.

Kachinas appear from about the time of the Winter Solstice in late December to Niman or the Home Dance in July. Particularly important in the sequence of these dances is Pamuya (Kiva Dances) in January, Powamu (Bean Dance) in February, Anktioni or Repeat Dances of March, and the Soyohim or Plaza Dances in April and May, with of course, Niman in July. Masked men perform in all of these rituals.

Although the Winter Solstice rites (called Soyal) emphasize such other matters as turning the sun back, they are also concerned with fertility and long life. At this time, late December, Chief Kachinas appear in the kivas "in the manner of sleepy early risers," says Wright. Other kachinas follow, for example, in January appear the Silent Warrior, Sio or Zuñi Shalako with his Sio Shalako Manas, and Saiastasa or the Zuñi Rain Priest of the North. The latter appears on First Mesa.

Then in February, at the well-known Bean Dance, many and varied kachinas come out of the kivas and perform in the plaza. This dance is held once every four years and is the time of the initiation of children into the kachina cult. It is also a time when beans are sprouted in the kivas in a short time—to the amazement of adults as well as children. Germination is stressed as well as the symbolizing of early stages of growth of corn and beans. The racing season opens now also, with objectives of both speeding growth and bringing rain.

More dances within the kivas follow in March. It is at this time that Eagle and Rooster Kachinas appear. When the weather becomes better in April and May, the Mixed Kachina Dances are presented in the plazas. Rain-bringing kachinas appear; they include the categories of Clouds, Other Indians, and Insects. All Hopis must be happy at this time, to insure rain and the fruition of all plants and animals. Three general types of kachinas appear in these plaza affairs: Line Dancers who are all the same kachinas; Mixed Dancers who are made up of a number of different kachinas; and Side Dancers who may appear with either of the preceding two but withdrawn from them.

The last of the kachina dances, Niman, is a time to say goodbye to all of the masked dancers. It is also a time to recognize the ripening of crops, particularly early corn. Gift giving by the kachinas, for example, the carved dolls to little girls, is a part of this ritual. Hopis offer prayers and thanks by tossing corn meal on the dancers.

Now the kachinas return to their mountain tops.

The actual number of kachinas among the Hopi Indians is unknown, but certain authorities have estimated that it is somewhere between 250 and 350. Some of the reasons for not knowing exactly how many include the facts that kachinas come and go, that old ones are dropped and new ones added, that some appear rarely, such as Hopi

Shalako. To add to the confusion, there are different versions of the same kachina which appear in different villages, plus the fact that individual carvers do not always remember the same details in a given kachina.

Not all of the kachinas are represented in the modern dolls. Some carvers are more conservative and would not represent certain ritual performers for they are too sacred to produce for sale. A relatively small number of dolls has become popular with both carver and buyer and these are done over and over. For example, the Clown is a widely favored piece.

Kachinas have been classified in several different ways. Wright, in his HOPI KACHINAS (above) gives the most logical and comprehensive classification of the few which have been offered. He bases his analysis on function, with some kachinas falling into several groups as they have varied functions. This is not a Hopi classification, although some of these tribesmen do recognize functional groups.

Below will be given the kachina dolls herein reproduced, with their connections with functional groups as established by Wright. This will aid in illustrating relationships between some kachinas. A word or two will also be said to indicate the functions of the groups cited.

The front cover presents one of the most important of the Chief or Mong Kachinas, Ahola. Chief Kachinas are closely associated with the basic Hopi social unit, the clan, in fact, they are thought of, in a sense, as the supernatural partners of the clan. Some of the other kachinas allied to the Chiefs are Crow Mother (page 16), Aholi and Eototo (both on page 20.)

One of the Great Ogres or Sosoyokt Kachina group is Black Nataska (page 1). This is a category of disciplinary kachinas. A week before they are to appear the Ogre Woman goes through the village telling all the little girls to grind corn and the little boys to catch mice, then she returns with the ugly Ogres who scorn the food the children have prepared and point out their other inadequacies. But parents come to their rescue, supporting their children, and giving food to the Ogres. Finally, the kachinas leave, with the children having learned that one must get along with his relatives and all must contribute to the food supply. Three others of the Sosoyokt group are White Ogre or Wiharu (pages 7 and 32), Chaveyo (page 10), and Awatovi Soyok Taka (page 11), all equally frightening in their hideous masks.

In a category titled Clowns and Non-Kachinas are included the un-masked Buffalo Dancer (page 5). Clowns are, however, the favored members of this group, reflecting the need for a lighter side to balance heavy ceremony. It is said that the Mudhead Clowns (pages 3, 22, 27) came from Zuñi, and that they indicate this by singing in the Zuñi language. Koshare (pages 7, 10, 18) are called Hano Clowns by the Hopi; many of their acts are quite vulgar. Two additional nonmasked members of this group are Snake Dancers or Chusona (page 14) and Poli Mana, the real Butterfly Girl (page 17), who is never masked; both have been popular for many years.

In the group, Kachina Women or Momoyam, is another Butterfly Girl, Palhik Mana (page 5) who does wear a mask on Third Mesa. These two, Poli and Palhik, are difficult to distinguish for the carver often puts a mask on Poli Mana, although occasionally she is represented without one. Hemis Kachin Mana (page 9) dances with different kachinas and merely changes her name accordingly—but not her dress. Two others in this group are Cold Bringing Woman (page 16) and Long Haired Kachina Girl (page 17). Many of the Momoyam wear the woman's dark dress, the red and black bordered white shawl, and the white buckskin boots of the Hopi woman.

Eagle (pages 6, 7) is one of the great Bird Kachinas or Chiro Kachinum group, and carvings of this personage are frequently executed for it is a favorite subject of the Hopis. Bird Kachinas play vital parts in many Hopi ceremonies. Owl (pages 21, 28) is also a great favorite, particularly the Great Horned Owl who is also a Warrior. Some birds "offer advice and council to the Hopis," thus showing how important this group is to the Indians.

Animals or Popkot Kachinas are also important to the Hopis for the members of this group are their "advisors, doctors and assistants," with, of course, other duties as well. Cow Kachina (page 7) for

instance, aids in cattle increase. Both curing and the bringing of rain are abilities of Mountain Sheep Kachina (page 8), and Hon or Bear Kachinas (pages 13, 26) may be white, black, or other colors; he is important as a doctor for he knows curative plants. Wolf Kachina (pages 24, 26) aids in hunting, while Antelope (page 31) appears with Wolf in Side Dances. Perhaps Badger (page 32) should be cited as the most important Animal Kachina for he is the outstanding curer.

Hopi Shalako Taka (page 8) belongs to the Mixed Kachinas or Sosoyohim Kachinum group. Some of these are concerned mainly with rain getting while others in the group are indirectly thus involved but give their first attention to other interests. Also, there is much over-lapping between these Mixed and other Kachinas. Hopi Shalako Taka "seems to represent all the Cloud People, and behaves more as a deity than a kachina."

The Plant Kachina group, or Tusak Kachinum is quite naturally of great importance to the Hopis. Through their dancing, these Kachinas literally "bring their own water." Corn is, of course, most important here for it has been the mainstay of life for the Hopis for centuries. Laguna Corn (page 11) is one of several types of these Kachinas among Hopi people. Another popular Plant Kachina is Squash, whose body looks quite like a melon but he carries identifying blossoms of the squash in his hands (page 27).

Two attractive Kachinas, Blue Ahote and Yellow Ahote, (page 12) belong to the Hunter or Mahk Kachinum group. This group is distinguished by the fact that its members are hunters of game, not of men, as are the Warriors, they are "soft" rather than "hard," and they are less ferocious in appearance. Left-Handed Kachina (page 27) belongs to this group...he does everything with the wrong hand. As might be expected, a variety of Bear Kachinas (page 26) belong here also and they are great and powerful.

Guard or Warrior Kachinas or Tuwalakum, are well represented by Zuñi Warrior God. Those in this group often carry yucca whips to fulfill their roles as protectors, warriors, and overseers, to keep people from certain ceremonial areas or events. Warrior Woman or He-e-e is one of the most interesting of Kachinas in this group: one aspect of her life is related under her photograph (page 19); another is that she is particularly involved in guarding certain ceremonies against the powers of other kachinas. Broad-Faced Kachina, (page 21) on the other hand, keeps He-e-e from getting too close during the Plumed Serpent Ceremony.

Early Morning Singer Kachina (page 23) is placed in the Miscellaneous Kachina group. Wright says this is "a group used merely to illustrate a few eccentricities." Sun Kachina (page 25) is also placed here; he does not dance in major performances. Some Hopis are vague about the purposes of attractively costumed Chasing Star or Meteor Kachina (page 30). Appearing in pairs, this dancer has a huge star on this face and wears a large feather headdress down his back.

A last group presented in these photographs is that of the Insect and Reptile Kachinas or the Sosoyohim Kachinum. Some within this group never go out of the kivas, for example the Water Serpent (page 22). Another member who has become more popular in recent years as a doll is Kokopelli or the Assassin Fly Kachina (page 29). Interestingly, these two, the Plumed Serpent and Kokopelli, are to be found widely in the Southwest among puebloans.

Thus it can be said that there is a wide variety of groups of kachinas among the Hopis, with their combined attributes covering all aspects of their world. Within each group are numerous kachinas with more individual traits, with many and varied gifts for the Hopis. Yet, withal, the bringing of rain is perhaps the most important of all. Each year the kachinas "help renew the world and ready it for the coming season of growth," each year they stand by to bring continued moisture and continued growth and an abundance of crops. Perhaps the Kachinas "greatest gift will be happiness, good health and a long life" for all the Hopi Indians.

Page 5, Number 3: Buffalo Dancer, left, who is not a kachina, and Palhik Mana, right, or Butterfly Girl who is masked on Third Mesa only. The real Butterfly Girl is not masked at all; despite this, carvers usually represent her with a mask.

Page 6, Number 4, left: Eagle Kachina, Kwahu. In the March Kiva Dance, these performers beautifully interpret this great bird. In this example the wings are carved of wood, whereas in other dolls often they were of real feathers. By Alvin James Makya.

Number 5, right: White Ogre, Wiharu. To frighten the children, these kachinas carry various items in their hands, this one a saw and bow and arrows—the better to frighten the children! By Cecil Calnimptewa.

Number 6, lower left: Eagle or Kwahu Kachina. This second Eagle is by Wilfred Tewawina. It is 36″ high which makes the two miniatures to the left seem even smaller—the latter, Eagle and Hano Clown, are by Mary Shelton. To the right is a medium-sized Mastop Kachina of Third Mesa.

Number 7, lower right: Cow or Wakas Kachina, left, and Koshare or Hano Clown, right. Cow Kachina dances for the increase of cattle; this is one of the later dolls, supposedly introduced around the turn of the century. Clown is by Wilfred Tewawina; he is amusing in his display of parasol in hand and pipe in mouth. Miniatures are Hemis Kachina, standing, by Mary Shelton, and Hemis Kachin' Mana, kneeling.

Number 8: left: Hopi Shalako Taka, Hopi Cloud Man, Cloud Person Male. Apparently Taka represents all of the cloud people; contrary to the Zuñi Shalakos who appear every year, this Hopi kachina is seen rarely in their villages. The Hopi Shalako also has a heavily feathered dress whereas the Zuñi dancer wears garments of woven cloth. By Alvin James Makya.

Page 9, Number 10, right: Hemis Mana, Kachina Girl, or Hemis Kachina Girl. As she comes out of the kiva she carries a gourd half shell and a sheep's scapula which she will play on a notched stick. By Lowell Talashoma.

Number 9, right: Mountain Sheep or Pong Kachina. Mountain Sheep Kachina appears in a group or line of dancers or sometimes alone in a Mixed Dance. He has power relative to rain and curing. By Alvin James Makya.

Page 10, Number 11, left: Chaveyo and Koshare Clown. These two tell of the disciplinary actions of Chaveyo, not only to children and men, but also to ceremonial performers. In this instance, Koshare clown has transgressed the rules of good conduct and is being taken to task by Chaveyo. Beautifully carved by Alvin James Makya.

Number 12, below: Laguna Corn Kachina or Sotung Taka. It is likely that this kachina first appeared at Hopi within the last twenty years; it is also possible that he came from Santo Domingo rather than Laguna.

Number 13, below: Awatovi Soyok' Taka. This doll resembles the Awatovi Ogre Man more than any other. Reputedly he acts like the White Nataska, and, like other Ogres, awaits the children with a basket on his back.

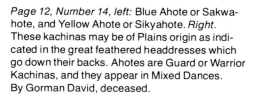

Page 12, Number 14, left: Blue Ahote or Sakwa-hote, and Yellow Ahote or Sikyahote. *Right.* These kachinas may be of Plains origin as indicated in the great feathered headdresses which go down their backs. Ahotes are Guard or Warrior Kachinas, and they appear in Mixed Dances. By Gorman David, deceased.

Number 15, above: Hon or Black Bear Kachina. There are many Bear Kachinas, all powerful, all can cure bad illnesses and all are very important as Warriors. By Neil David.

Number 16, left: Detail of head of Hon or Bear Kachina. Notable are the fur, the vicious mouth, and the glaring eyes.

Number 17, above: Snake Dancers, Chusona. The right figure is the Snake Carrier and the left is a "Hugger" who follows close to the first and helps him if the need arises. Although not a kachina, the Snake Dancer is a very popular doll. The performer's face is painted—he does not wear a mask. These dancers appear in August to assure the late rains for maturation of crops. Dolls by Henry Shelton.

Page 15, Number 18, right: Zuñi Warrior or Talamopaiyakya, a Zuñi kachina which is undergoing change by the Hopis. As he dances very fast, his part is taken by younger men only. Perhaps because he comes in all directional colors and is relatively simple in mask and dress, he is a favorite of kachina carvers. He is a Guard Kachina as partially indicated in his yucca whips. By Alvin James Makya.

Number 20, left: Koshare or Hano Clown, Paiyakyamu, Glutton. These plus other names, would indicate that this clown may be found in many different pueblos. Also they are contrary characters in that they may perform sacred or profane actions, some of the latter embarrassing to the gathered people.

Number 21, below: Koshare. This fellow is like a koshare in his unmasked face and in his hair-do, but his body is painted somewhat like that of a Koyemsi. His dress follows that of neither. By Fletcher Healing. To the far left is an Owl Kachina.

Number 22: He'e'e or Warrior Maiden Kachina. Two stories prevail regarding this powerful Kachina. One tells of a man exchanging clothes with his bride when enemies approached. Another tells of a girl surprised by attackers so she picks up her father's weapons and successfully defends her village. In either case, the hairdress has been but half completed, with one whorl up at the side of the head, the rest of the hair loose—and thus the warrior maiden is represented, complete with bow in one hand. Carving by Alvin James Makya.

Page 20, Number 23: Aholi *(left)* and Eototo *(right)* Kachinas. Aholi is Kachina Chief's Lieutenant; he appears in ceremonies on Third Mesa only. His many colored "cloak," with a Germ God on the back, represents flowers and "the brightness of summer." Eototo, who is chief of all the kachinas, controls the seasons and may appear in any of the ceremonies for he knows all of them. Both kachinas by Cecil Calnimptewa.

Number 24, above: Great Horned Owl or Mongwu. An often-produced kachina, this owl is usually very well made; particularly are the feathers so well carved and painted that they could be nothing but those of the owl. As a warrior kachina, the Great Horned Owl keeps the Clowns from going too far in their antics. By Wilfred Tewawina.

Number 25, right: Broad-Faced Kachina, or Wuyak-kuita, is another Guard who appears on all three mesas; on each he has slightly different duties. For example, on Second and Third Mesas he takes care of the great line of dancers at the Bean Dance. On First Mesa he enters with Ogre Women. By Ira Tewawina.

Page 22, Number 26, left: Palolokong is the Water or Plumed Serpent. There is a kachina of this Serpent who never appears outside the kiva. Hahai-i Wuhti (Kachina Mother or Grandmother), Badger and Parrot Kachinas among others appear in the Water Serpent ceremony; here, obviously, are three Koyemsi with the two Snakes.

Number 27, above: Early Morning Singer or Talavai Kachina. Strangely, he is also called Silent Kachina. Note that about his shoulders is a maiden's white shawl with red and dark blue or black borders—Wright says that many kachinas who appear in the early morning wear this robe. Talavai appears in The Bean Dance. By Wilfred Tewawina.

Page 24, Number 28, left: Wolf or Kweo, a hunter Kachina. This photograph illustrates the unifinished or whitewashed stage (right) before the doll is painted, with the completed doll to the left. In older dolls Kweo is like this one, but many newer ones are bedecked with fur covering the head, with greater teeth, and tongue hanging out. He is a Side Dancer in Soyohim. By Gorman David.

Number 29, above: Sun, Tawa. Interestingly, Sun Kachina is not seen in any important performances, but rather, appears as an average personage in the Mixed Dance. The beautiful pottery plate decorated with the Sun design is by Thomas Nampeyo.

Number 30, left: Another Wolf or Kweo appears as a side dancer along with Deer and Antelope Kachinas. Kweo is offered prayer feathers and corn meal so that he will aid the Indians in securing game. There is excellent detail in this miniature carving. By Myron Gaseoma.

Page 27, Number 32, right: Three favorite kachinas, Left Handed (top) by Lowell Talashoma. Squash (lower left), and a Mudhead (lower right), the latter two by Ronald Honyouti. Left Handed, (Siyangaphoya) has everything reversed, yet he is a fine hunter. Squash or Patung is a Chief Kachina and a runner on First Mesa; squash blossoms on his head and in his hands identify him. This Mudhead or Koyemsi is busily carving a kachina doll.

Number 31, right; Bear or Hon Kachina. Of the many Bear Kachinas, some are distinguished by color alone, such as Blue, or Yellow, or this White Bear. Most frequently these Kachinas appear in Mixed Dances. The bear's great strength is reflected in his ability to cure. By Arthur Holmes.

Number 33: Mongwu Kachina or Great Horned Owl is also a Guard or Warrior Kachina who carries whips with which he asserts his authority when necessary, particularly over clowns. They also serve in the capacity of protectors and overseers. By Cliff Bahnimptewa.

Number 34: Kokopelli is also known as Assassin Fly Kachina or Humpbacked Flute Player. He may appear alone in Mixed Dances or with others of his type in Kiva Dances. The Humpbacked Flute Player was a popular subject for prehistoric artists of the Southwest, seemingly then as now associated with fertility. By Alvin James Makya.

Number 35, left: Chasing Star, Nangasohu, or Meteor Kachina. He has a great four-pointed star covering most of his face mask and an equally great headpiece falling down his back. Meteor Kachinas attend the Mixed Dance in pairs. Beautifully carved by Peter Shelton.

Right: Field Mouse. This character does not exist, neither as a kachina nor a dancer among the Hopis. However, because of a request for Field Mouse who went to war as told in a story, he was produced as a doll. Requests for Mickey Mouse have resulted in his reproduction despite the fact that he, too, has never appeared in a Hopi dance. By Gorman David.

Number 36, above: Antelope or Chop Kachinas. This kachina may appear as an individual dancer or with other kachinas. He aids in bringing rain and in making the grass grow. These two representations are quite similar. Left figure by Peter Shelton, right by Narron Lomayaktewa.

Number 37, left: This version of Badger carries a bow in his right hand, a rattle in the left, and has badger tracks on his cheeks. A curing kachina, he appears in both Powamu and Pachavi ceremonies.

Right: White Ogre. When he appears with other ugly kachinas, all growling and stamping, little boys proffer mice and little girls ground corn. Refused, the children offer more, eventually providing enough so that the Ogres depart. Bow and arrows in his left hand also indicate hunting. By Narron Lomayaktewa.